W9-AMN-432

KAWHI LEONARD

Jon M. Fishman

Lerner Publications ◆ Minneapolis

Lerner Publications Company
A division of Lerner Publishing Group, Inc.
241 First Avenue North
Minneapolis, MN 55401 USA

For reading levels and more information, look up this title at www.lernerbooks.com.

Main body text set in Albany Std 15/22. Typeface provided by Agfa.

Library of Congress Cataloging-in-Publication Data

Names: Fishman, Jon M., author.
Title: Kawhi Leonard / Jon M. Fishman.
Description: Minneapolis, Minnesota : Lerner Publications, [2018] | Series: Sports
    All-Stars | Includes webography. | Includes bibliographical references and index. |
    Audience: Ages: 7–11. | Audience: Grades: 4 to 6.
Identifiers: LCCN 2017035885 (print) | LCCN 2017039874 (ebook) |
    ISBN 9781541500433 (eb pdf) | ISBN 9781541500419 (library binding : alk.
    paper) | ISBN 9781541512030 (paperback : alk. paper)
Subjects: LCSH: Leonard, Kawhi, 1991—Juvenile literature. | Basketball players—
    United States—Biography—Juvenile literature. | San Antonio Spurs (Basketball
    team—History—Juvenile literature.
Classification: LCC GV884.L465 (ebook) | LCC GV884.L465 F57 2018 (print) | DDC
    796.323092 [B]—c23

LC record available at https://lccn.loc.gov/2017035885

Manufactured in the United States of America
1-43666-33482-10/3/2017

CONTENTS

SAN ANTONIO
SUPERSTAR

Kawhi Leonard fights past a Houston Rockets defender to get to the ball.

Kawhi Leonard of the San Antonio Spurs was struggling to score against the Houston Rockets. He made just one basket in the first quarter. Then he missed four shots in a row. Missing so many shots would discourage some players. But Leonard didn't let it get to him. He knows he is a superstar in the National Basketball Association (NBA).

Leonard and the Spurs were playing in the 2017 NBA **playoffs**. The seven-game series was tied—each team had won one game. Both teams were desperate to win game 3 and take the series lead.

The beginning of the second quarter wasn't much better for Leonard. He missed his first shot. Then a Rockets player jumped to **block** his second shot. The Spurs were losing, 26–23.

Leonard kept working hard. He played tough defense against Rockets superstar James Harden. Before long, Leonard started scoring. He threw down a powerful **slam dunk**.

Leonard moves around a defender during a playoff game against Houston.

Then he made a shot from about 10 feet (3 m) from the basket. He knocked down **layups** and **free throws**. San Antonio had the lead at halftime, 43–39.

Leonard kept scoring in the second half. He made baskets from all around the court, including two **three-point shots**. San Antonio won the game, 103–92. Leonard scored 26 points. He also grabbed 10 **rebounds**. "We started off pretty slow, but I think we did good," he said.

Leonard jumps for a slam dunk against the Houston Rockets.

Houston won the next game in the series. In game 5, Leonard twisted his ankle when he stepped on James Harden's foot. The Spurs won, but Leonard sat on the bench for the last part of the game. He didn't play at all in game 6. San Antonio managed to win without him to take the series victory.

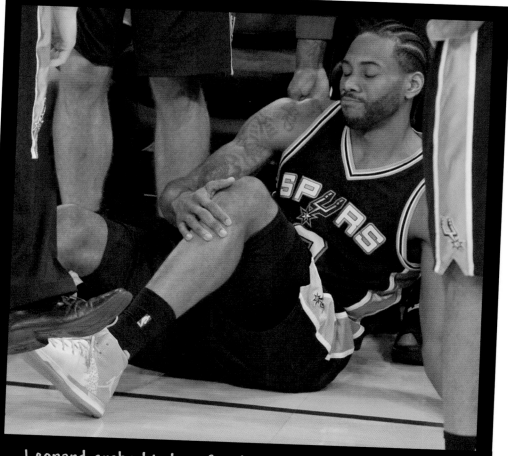

Leonard grabs his leg after becoming injured in a game.

Leonard watches from the bench as the Spurs play against the Golden State Warriors in the playoffs.

In the next round of the playoffs, the Spurs played the Golden State Warriors. Leonard's ankle was feeling better, but he hurt it again in the first game against Golden State. He left the game and couldn't play again in the series. The Warriors **swept** the Spurs in four games.

Leonard was disappointed in the way the 2016–2017 season ended. But it had been his best year in the league. He averaged more than 27 points and almost eight rebounds per game. He finished third in the voting for NBA Most Valuable Player (MVP). The Spurs will have many more chances in the playoffs with Leonard leading the way.

Kawhi handles the ball during a high school basketball game.

Kawhi Leonard was born on June 29, 1991, in Riverside, California. Riverside is near Los Angeles. He grew up with his father, Mark, and his mother, Kim. Kawhi has four older sisters.

Kawhi was a smart boy who had many interests.

He enjoyed math, especially **geometry**. His favorite sport was basketball. "I could be on the court for two hours and it felt like 10 minutes," he said. He loved basketball so much that when he was seven years old, he predicted that he would play in the NBA someday.

His path to the NBA became a little rocky when he was a high school freshman. His parents were working, and he couldn't find a ride to his high school basketball team's **tryouts**. He couldn't be on the team if he didn't take part in the tryouts. Kawhi decided to play football that year instead. He was back on the basketball team for his sophomore season, and he was quickly growing into a powerful force on the court.

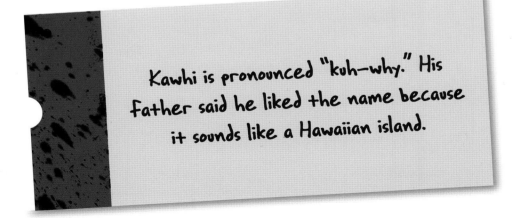

Kawhi is pronounced "kuh-why." His father said he liked the name because it sounds like a Hawaiian island.

During Kawhi's junior season, tragedy struck. His father was shot and killed at the car wash he owned in Compton, California. No one knew who shot him or why.

Just hours after learning of his father's death, Kawhi played in a basketball game. He played well despite the sad news. After the game, he cried with his mother. The sport he loved helped him deal with his family's loss. "Basketball helps me take my mind off things, picking me up every day when I'm feeling down," Kawhi said.

Kawhi dunks the ball on an outdoor court in Riverside, California.

Kawhi reaches for the basket in a high school game.

Kawhi was one of the best high school basketball players in the United States by his senior season. In 2009, he averaged 22.6 points and 13.1 rebounds per game. Basketball coaches voted him California Mr. Basketball. That meant the coaches thought Kawhi was the best high school player in the state.

After high school, Leonard stayed in California to play at San Diego State University. He averaged more than 14 points and 10 rebounds per game for the team. In 2011, he entered the NBA **Draft**. The Indiana Pacers chose Leonard with the 15th overall pick. Then they traded him to San Antonio. Leonard had achieved his lifelong dream of playing in the NBA.

Leonard (*center*) jumps to block a pass in a 2009 college game.

Leonard stretches out his long arms to block a shot by Matt Barnes.

Kawhi Leonard is 6 feet 7 inches (2 m) tall. The distance from the tip of a player's left hand to the tip of the right hand when the arms are held straight out is called wingspan. Kawhi's wingspan is 7 feet 3 inches (2.2 m). That's about 4.5 inches (11 cm) longer than the wingspan of most people his height. His hands are also bigger than usual.

Leonard reaches out to block a shot during a 2017 game against the Houston Rockets.

Long arms and big hands help Leonard on the basketball court. He can reach higher for rebounds. Other players have a hard time getting shots past him. Leonard's arms and hands are natural gifts that have helped him become a superstar. But he works awfully hard to take advantage of those gifts.

In college, Leonard often awoke at five o'clock to exercise before classes. He would work out for up to seven hours each day. "We've never had a guy that's put more gym time in when nobody's watching, when it's not required," said Steve Fisher, Leonard's college coach.

Leonard's desire to work and improve is one of the reasons the Spurs wanted him to join the team. The team immediately set out to make him an even better player.

Leonard sets up to take a shot during a practice.

They showed him videos of NBA legends such as Kobe Bryant. Leonard watched Bryant's shooting style and tried to copy it. Spurs coach Gregg Popovich said Leonard often stayed in the gym after practice to work on **jump shots** and other moves.

In 2012, Leonard twisted his knee and missed 18 games. He took time to heal and make sure the injury wouldn't happen again. He did exercises such as running backward over a speed ladder. A speed ladder looks like a flat ladder on the ground. He twisted his hips and stepped quickly through the ladder. The exercises strengthened his legs and improved how well he could run sideways and backward.

Leonard stretches his legs during practice.

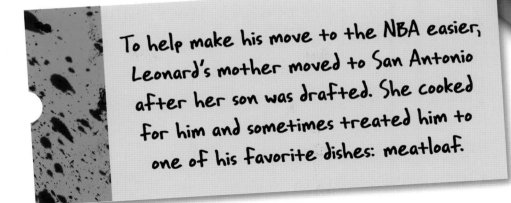

To help make his move to the NBA easier, Leonard's mother moved to San Antonio after her son was drafted. She cooked for him and sometimes treated him to one of his favorite dishes: meatloaf.

Leonard usually eats a healthful diet to make sure he's getting the most out of his workouts. He avoids fast food and sugary snacks. Chicken, fish, fruit, and lots of vegetables are on his menu. He also drinks a lot of water. Wholesome food gives Leonard the energy he needs to keep up with the world's best basketball players.

CLAW

Leonard practices shooting to prepare for a game.

Leonard's friends and teammates know him as a quiet person. He doesn't brag or talk a lot. He puts all his energy into getting ready for games, and he plays with passion every second he's on the court. Then he usually heads home to watch TV. Or he might spend a quiet evening with friends and family.

Rather than talking about himself, Leonard expresses

Leonard hugs his mom, Kim, after a game.

himself in other ways. In 2016, he and the sportswear company Nike began selling a collection of clothing. Leonard helped design the T-shirts, hats, and sweatshirts himself. The items each feature an image of a large hand. Kawhi came up with the idea for the hand because his own hands are so large. The image goes well with the nickname Leonard's teammates gave him: the Claw.

Leonard wears a hat and shirt featuring the image he created at an event in 2017.

Leonard earns money from the clothing he designed, but he makes a lot more playing basketball. As a **rookie** in 2011–2012, he made almost $2 million with the Spurs. He didn't rush out and spend the money. He kept driving the same car that he'd driven in college—a Chevy Malibu. He eventually bought a fancier car, but he still kept the Malibu.

When Leonard was voted the NBA Defensive Player of the Year for the 2014–2015 season, he got another new car. It was part of his reward for the honor. But he gave the car to Respite Care of San Antonio, a group that helps children in need in the area.

Giving away a brand-new car is just one of the things Leonard has done to help people. He works with the Ronald McDonald House to improve the lives of children.

Leonard holds up his Defensive Player of the Year award.

TV Star

It's common to see Leonard on TV, and not just in basketball games. He's appeared on many sports interview shows. Once he was a guest on *Live! with Kelly and Michael*. He talked with the hosts about his NBA career and dealing with losses. They even shot some baskets!

Fans love Leonard's TV commercials for the H-E-B supermarket chain. He and his teammates have appeared in a series of funny ads for the company. They joke around and have fun. In one ad, Leonard makes a giant snowball out of paper. In another, he uses his huge hands to get his laundry done quickly.

In 2016, he donated sneakers to a high school basketball team in Riverside. That same year, he dressed up as Santa Claus and delivered presents to kids in San Antonio. The Spurs posted a photo on Twitter of Leonard in his Santa suit with the caption, "Guess who!"

"JUST THE BEGINNING"

Tim Duncan (*left*) and Leonard run up the court during a 2012 game.

The San Antonio Spurs were a good team when Kawhi Leonard joined them in 2011–2012. But their longtime superstar, Tim Duncan, was nearing the end of his incredible career. The Spurs knew they would soon need someone to step in and become the new leader of the team.

Leonard celebrates with his teammates after being named NBA Finals MVP.

By the 2013–2014 season, Leonard had become that leader. He guided the team to a regular season record of 62–20. Then he helped the Spurs capture the NBA championship. Leonard averaged 14 points per game in the playoffs and played great defense. He was voted NBA Finals MVP.

He was even better the next season when he was voted NBA Defensive Player of the Year. The Spurs rewarded him with a **contract** that would pay him more than $94 million over five seasons. Leonard didn't let his riches slow him down. He worked just as hard as ever, and he keeps getting better. His points-per-game average has risen each year he's been in the league.

Leonard was voted to the NBA All-Star Game in 2016 and 2017. When one of his former college coaches heard the news, he sent Leonard a message to say congratulations. "Thanks," Leonard said. "This is just the beginning."

The Spurs have been one of the NBA's most successful teams in recent years. They won the NBA Finals in 1999, 2003, 2005, 2007, and 2014. They made it to the Finals in 2013 but lost to LeBron James and the Miami Heat.

All-Star Stats

In 2014–2015, Kawhi Leonard, then 23, was one of the youngest players to win the **NBA** Defensive Player of the Year Award. He won it again in 2015–2016. Take a look at the youngest players to ever win the award:

NBA Defensive Players of the Year by Age

Player	Age
Kawhi Leonard (2014–2015)	23
Dwight Howard (2008–2009)	23
Alvin Robertson (1985–1986)	23
Kawhi Leonard (2015–2016)	24
Dwight Howard (2009–2010)	24
Metta World Peace (2003–2004)	24
Michael Jordan (1987–1988)	24
Dwight Howard (2010–2011)	25
Sidney Moncrief (1982–1983)	25

Source Notes

7   Associated Press, "Aldridge Steps Up to Help Spurs Down Rockets 103–92," *ESPN*, May 6, 2017, http://www.espn.com/nba/recap?gameId=400952492.

11 Lee Jenkins, "The Island of Kawhi: Leonard Gives Second Wind to Spurs' Dynasty," *Sports Illustrated*, March 14, 2016, https://www.si.com/nba/2016/03/15/kawhi-leonard-spurs-tim-duncan-gregg-popovich-tony-parker-manu-ginobili.

12 Eric Sondheimer, "Shooting Death of His Father Drives Riverside King's Leonard," *Los Angeles Times*, March 8, 2008, http://www.latimes.com/sports/la-sp-sondheimer8mar08-column.html.

17 Ben Bolch, "Spurs' Kawhi Leonard Has Prevailed in Tough Times," *Los Angeles Times*, June 11, 2014, http://www.latimes.com/sports/la-sp-heat-spurs-nba-finals-20140612-story.html.

24 Dana Scott, "Kawhi Leonard Dressed Up as Santa Claus and Delivered Gifts to Kids for Spurs Holiday Drive," *Complex*, December 17, 2016, http://www.complex.com/sports/2016/12/kawhi-leonard-dressed-up-as-santa-claus-delivering-gifts-to-kids-spurs-holiday-drive.

27 Tom Haberstroh, "Devotion to the Data: How Kawhi Leonard Became a Superstar," *ESPN*, February 24, 2016, http://www.espn.com/nba/story/_/id/14763202/how-biometrics-turned-kawhi-leonard-star.

Glossary

block: to slap a shot away from the basket

contract: an agreement between a player and a team that states how much the player will be paid and for how long

draft: an event in which teams take turns choosing new players

free throws: unguarded shots from the free-throw line

geometry: a type of math that deals with angles, lines, and planes

jump shots: shots taken after jumping off the court

layups: one-handed shots near the basket

playoffs: a series of games played at the end of a season to decide a champion

rebounds: balls that bounce away from the basket after missed shots

rookie: a first-year player

slam dunk: a shot made by jumping in the air near the basket and throwing the ball through the hoop

swept: won every game in a series

three-point shots: shots from behind the three-point line on each end of the court

tryouts: tests of players' abilities to see if they will become members of a team

Fishman, Jon M. *James Harden*. Minneapolis: Lerner Publications, 2016.

Fishman, Jon M. *LeBron James*. Minneapolis: Lerner Publications, 2018.

Jr. NBA
https://jr.nba.com

Kawhi Leonard
http://www.nba.com/players/kawhi/leonard/202695

San Antonio Spurs
http://www.nba.com/spurs

Whiting, Jim. *San Antonio Spurs*. Mankato, MN: Creative Education, 2017.

Index

Photo Acknowledgments

The images in this book are used with the permission of: Jayne Kamin-Oncea/Getty Images, p. 2 (background); Ronald Martinez/Getty Images, pp. 4–5, 6, 7, 16; Jose Carlos Fajardo/TNS/Newscom, p. 8; Soobum Im/USA Today Sports/Newscom, pp. 9, 23; Louis Lopez/Cal Sport Media/Newscom, p. 10; Gina Ferazzi/Los Angeles Times/Getty Images, p. 12; Richard Hartog/Los Angeles Times/Getty Images, p. 13; Derrick Tuskan/Icon SMI/Newscom, p. 14; Frederick Breedon/Getty Images, p. 15; AP Photo/Lynne Sladky, p. 17; Alex Trautwig/Getty Images, p. 18; AP Photo/Rick Bowmer, p. 20; AP Photo/David J. Phillip, p. 21; Visual China Group/Getty Images, p. 22; Chris Szagola/Cal Sport Media/Newscom, p. 25; MIKE STONE/REUTERS/Newscom, p. 26.

Cover: Jayne Kamin-Oncea/Getty Images.